Building a
Partnership
With Your Boss

Building a Partnership With Your Boss

A Take-Charge Assistant Book

Jerry Wisinski

AMACOM

American Management Association International
New York • Atlanta • Boston • Kansas City • San Francisco • Washington, D.C.
Brussels • Mexico City • Tokyo • Toronto

Library of Congress Cataloging-in-Publication Data

Wisinski, Jerry.
    Building a partnership with your boss : a take-charge assistant book/Jerry Wisinski
      p. cm.
    Includes index.
    ISBN 0-8144-7013-0
    1. Managing your boss.   2. Administrative assistants.
   3. Secretaries.   I. Title.
   HF5548.83.W57   1999
   650.1'3—dc21   98-49846
                                                        CIP

Printing number

10 9 8 7 6 5 4 3 2 1

Contents

*To my
family*

Building a
Partnership
With Your Boss

Introduction

Over the past years, the working relationship between executive secretaries and administrative assistants with their bosses has changed dramatically. What used to be a "working for" concept has changed to a "working with" proposition.

Today it has gone even further. Now, "partnershipping" is rapidly becoming the norm among bosses and their key employees. No longer are secretaries and administrative assistants seen as errand runners or typists. Rather they are now reliable and essential partners with their bosses.

This book offers you the framework for developing an effective working partnership with your boss. Covering the key issues encountered in work relationships, it gives you a commonsense, step-by-step process necessary to developing the partnership concept into your reality. In addition, each chapter includes a brief summary for easy reference.

After you've finished reading through this book, give it to your boss for his or her review. Better yet, buy another one—one for you and one for your boss.

Developing an effective working partnership requires time; it won't happen overnight. But the growth and rewards you and your boss will experience will certainly make the effort worth the time.

Good reading, and here's to your partnership.

1

Understanding the
Business Partnership Concept

Yesterday

Once upon a time, secretaries and bosses had a rather lopsided relationship.

She took dictation in shorthand, typed, filed, answered the phone, ran personal errands (typically his), and made coffee for everyone attending important meetings. She may have even washed windows and mopped the floor.

He acted like the typical boss, telling her what to do and when, often not explaining what he wanted clearly, but expecting her to read his mind. He was the lord of the office, often taking the credit for both his efforts and hers. Of course, he didn't know how to make coffee.

So much for yesterday.

Today

Times have changed. Today the relationship between bosses and secretaries is much more balanced, team-oriented, and moving increasingly toward a partnership concept. It's not unusual for an executive secretary or administrative assistant to be an integral part of those important meetings, be consulted by her boss on critical matters, be empowered to run projects, lead a team, or even manage others.

Hopefully the working relationship you have with your boss is more representative of today's profile rather than yesterday's. Additionally, the movement today is toward developing a working partnership between bosses and their secretaries or administrative assistants.

The Partnership Model

Following is a model showing the different stages in relationship development between bosses and secretaries that led to the partnership concept. After reading the explanations, you should be able to identify where your relationship with your boss is now and where you would like it to be.

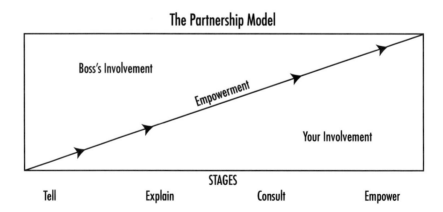

The Four Stages
of the Boss/Secretary
Relationship Development

At first glance it may seem as though the only stages useful in the partnership concept are the Consult and Empowerment stages. However, this isn't true; the four stages are situational, with each appropriate at different times in maintaining a good relationship.

1 The Tell Stage

In the Tell stage, your boss considers a situation, makes a decision, and informs you of the result. There is little to no discussion.

Historically, the Tell stage was typical of the relationship between bosses and their secretaries. He would tell; she would do.

Working for someone who overuses the Tell style isn't exactly fun. However, when it is used appropriately, it becomes understandable and has little to no negative effect.

When Telling Is Appropriate

- When singular decisions must be made
- When unpopular policies need to be implemented
- When time is of the essence

2 The Explain Stage

In the Explain stage, your boss considers a situation, makes a decision, informs you of the result, and is willing to explain the reasons and entertain questions and discussion.

Although the Explain stage is only one level higher than Tell, it is typically seen as a more positive way of informing you of decisions that must be carried out. Most of us prefer being told why we need to do something rather than simply being told to do it.

When Explaining Is Appropriate

- When implementing something new
- When commitment is important
- When attempting to sell a new idea

3 The Consult Stage

In the Consult stage your boss presents a situation to you, asks for your thoughts, and makes a decision based on a combination of both your and his or her information.

Good things begin happening in the Consult Stage. First, it makes you feel positive knowing your feedback is valuable. Second, it motivates you to want to contribute more. Finally, it signifies a natural beginning stage in developing the business partnership with your boss.

When Consulting Is Appropriate

- When there is a level of trust beginning to develop between you and your boss
- When your boss recognizes your expertise in certain areas
- When the partnership concept is in its early stages

4 The Empowerment Stage

In the Empowerment stage, your boss presents you with a situation, indicates his or her faith in you, and gives you the authority to make the necessary decisions to see the situation through.

When Empowering Is Appropriate

Empowerment and the business partnership go hand in hand. It implies that you and your boss have developed a level of mutual trust, respect, and high expectations of each other. Typically this results in a highly motivated environment, with you feeling that your efforts are an integral part of the work being accomplished.

Both you and your boss must take certain specific steps in order for Empowerment to be successful, particularly in the area of giving responsibility and determining authority. More on this later.

- When there is a level of high trust between the two of you
- When you are ready for additional responsibility
- When your boss is willing to have you represent him or her

Although both the Consulting and Empowerment stages are critical to developing the business partnership, the reality is that all four stages are necessary in maintaining a good working relationship. Sometimes your boss must call the shots; at other times you can be empowered to make the decisions.

The big question is this: *At which of the four stages does your boss tend to manage you?* If it is predominantly at the Tell or Explain stage, you will have a difficult time developing a partnership. If it is mainly at the Consult or Empowerment level, you are already on the way to developing a strong business partnership.

The Triangles

One of the dynamics of the partnership model is continual movement left and right along the scale according to the situation. The rectangle above the scale is composed of two triangles: one representing your boss's involvement, the other representing yours.

With the Tell and Explain styles, there is heavy involvement on your boss's part and little involvement on yours. Your boss is making the decisions, perhaps checking on you often, and you're doing the work. As you move into the Consult stage and toward the Empowerment stage, you become more involved in the decision process, allowing your boss to manage indirectly while you become more directly involved. In other words, your activity increases while your boss's activity decreases.

The common diagonal line joining both triangles indicates an increase or decrease in motivation. Movement toward the right results in higher degrees; movement toward the left results in the opposite effect. In theory, the more involved you are in the decision-making process, the higher your level of motivation.

Two Critical Elements in Developing the Business Partnership

There are two key elements necessary to developing the partnership: your boss and you. Consider the following questions relating to the partnership model:

Your Boss

- Does your boss frequently consult with you on important issues?
- Is he or she able to give you an assignment and then let you complete it without continual interference?
- Does your boss give you credit privately and in front of others?
- Are you ever asked to represent him or her or the department at meetings?
- Have you been asked to serve as a team member or leader?

You

- Are you good at prioritizing your job tasks?
- Are you willing and able to accept higher levels of responsibilities?
- Do you attempt to increase your value to your boss?
- Do you offer solutions to situations when they arise?
- Do you ask your boss if you can help on projects outside your job description?

The more you can answer yes to these questions about your boss and you, the closer the two of you are to beginning or enhancing the development of the business partnership. Of course, there's more to it than that. The following chapters give you the information necessary to developing the foundation for this relationship.

Summary

The working dynamics between bosses and secretaries has changed dramatically over the years. Today the concept is to develop a partnership to strengthen the working relationship.

In developing this partnership with your boss, use the partnership model to determine the progress that both of you are making.

If you weren't able to answer yes to some of the questions about your boss and you, focus on these areas to help improve the partnering relationship.

2

Initiating the Transition

Establishing the business partnership requires a concerted effort by both you and your boss; you can't do it on your own. You can prepare yourself by considering where you might be willing to adapt before you present the idea. A good starting point is to consider the work values the two of you have in common and where you may have differences.

Work Values

Our work values are an outgrowth of our core value system developed during our childhood, adolescence, and young adult stages of life. Our value system acts as a filter through which we see the world. It helps us to decide how we should behave, judge right or wrong, even choose acquaintances, friends, and loving relationships. For example, we typically choose friends based on mutual discovery of common interests and beliefs we judge to be compatible. Conversely, we tend not to remain acquainted with those not having values common with our own. In social life, it's our decision; in professional life, we don't always have the luxury of choice.

It would be wonderful if we could choose the boss, peers, and other associates with whom we would like to work. So much for fantasy. In reality, we may have to work for a boss or with others that have different work values from ours.

10

When establishing the business partnership, it is important to determine what your boss's work values are and where you are able to adapt to those values.

Unstated Expectations

Work values carry with them unstated expectations of others; that is, unconsciously, we expect others to see things the way we see them. More specifically, your boss probably expects you to understand and act in accordance with his or her values.

Examples

- If your boss has a place for everything and everything in its place, what do you think the unstated expectation is for your work space?
- If your boss is detail-oriented and writes everything down, what do you think the unstated expectation is when you present an idea?

Following are some questions to help you analyze your boss's work style. Consider them carefully and answer them purely from his or her point of view *regardless of your personal feelings*.

Questionnaire
Analyzing Your Boss's Work Style

1. *What is your boss's work schedule?* Arrive early and leave late? Arrive on time and leave on time? Go to lunch, bring lunch, work through lunch? _____

   What would be the unstated expectation? _____

   _____

   _____

(continued)

(continued)

2. *What is the appearance of your boss's office?* Is there a place for everything and everything in its place? Is there a homey feel or a strictly business atmosphere? _____

   What would be the unstated expectation? _____

   _____

   _____

3. *Is he or she bottom-line oriented or detail-oriented?* Does he or she get to the main point quickly or give a lot of background information?

   _____

   What would be the unstated expectation? _____

   _____

   _____

4. *Does your boss tend to document messages or deliver them orally?*

   _____

   What would be the unstated expectation?

   _____

   _____

5. *When is your boss's prime work time?* At what time of the day does your boss seem to be most productive in accomplishing tasks? _____

   _____

What would be the unstated expectation?

_____

_____

6. *When is your boss most receptive to you?* Is it during prime work time, or at another time during the day? _____

_____

_____

What would be the unstated expectation?

_____

_____

After carefully considering these questions and the unstated expectations, ask yourself the critical question: *Where are you willing to adapt your work values to fit the values your boss has without losing your individual sense of self?*

Establishing a business partnership does require certain changes, but it doesn't mean losing your identity or completely rearranging how you work. Ideally, both you and your boss should be flexible enough to develop mutually acceptable work habits. If you can pull that off—wonderful. If not, you need to be willing to adapt your work style (where possible) to fit your boss's in order to lay the foundation for establishing the business partnership.

Following is an actual situation. After reading the situation, answer the questions that follow.

Case Study

Gerri is the office manager for a consulting firm owned by her boss, Judy. Gerri is high key; she likes to get to work early and leave on time. She is bottom-line-oriented, likes to present ideas orally rather than in writing, and is most productive early in the morning. Her desk is always clean, and she takes pride in maintaining a professional decor in her work area.

Judy, her boss, is laid back. She arrives at the office between 9 A.M. and 10 A.M. and usually stays until 7 P.M. or 8 P.M. Her office is messy by Gerri's standards: piles of papers stacked high on her desk and credenza, photographs and mementos of her travels everywhere else. Judy likes to consider issues for a while before making decisions and is detail-oriented, preferring documentation to help her in the decision-making process.

Although there is some tension between the two, there is also a high level of respect for each other's abilities. Recently, Gerri attended a presentation that focused on partnershipping with your boss. She liked the idea and wants to approach Judy with the concept.

1. What work values do you think Gerri should be willing to change in order to lay a good foundation for developing a partnership with Judy?

   _____

   _____

2. What work values do you think she should keep as they are?

   _____

   _____

3. What other suggestions would you have for the two of them that would help in developing this relationship?

_____

_____

Suggestion

You may want to use this case study as a model for you and your boss to begin the process of partnershipping. If you don't think your boss can participate at this time, you can still do the following on your own:

- Objectively describe your work values on a sheet of paper. Use your first name rather than I to help you remain objective.
- Describe your boss's work values using his or her first name, also to help you remain objective.
- Based on your objective analysis of both individuals, make a list of suggestions indicating where (*your name*) could adapt work values in order to improve the relationship.
- List the values (*your name*) should keep as they are and the reason(s) why.

This exercise should give you a good insight into some primary considerations before you present the partnership idea to your boss.

To be honest, partnershipping isn't for everyone.

Although partnershipping requires change by both parties, *you* will be primarily responsible for initiating the concept and maintaining its continued development.

Summary

Both you and your boss have work values. Sometimes these are clearly expressed, and other times they are unstated expectations.

To establish an effective partnership with your boss, it's important for you to know his or her values. Such things as work schedules, preferring written or oral reports, and knowing the best time to approach your boss with issues are important considerations in working with your boss more effectively.

The more you are willing to adapt to his or her preferences while still maintaining your own work values, the stronger your partnership will become.

3

The Beginning Steps

"How About Developing a Partnership?"

Once you've analyzed your boss's work values and where you're willing to adapt, you're ready to propose developing the partnership.

When presenting the concept, consider the following important elements in your proposal:

- What's in it for him or her (WIIFH).
- What's in it for you.
- There is an ongoing process involved.
- There are specific areas that will help establish the working partnership.
- Both you and your boss will have individual responsibilities in each area.

If your boss agrees to these elements, you're ready to forge ahead.

So What Do We Do First?

Begin the partnership process by discussing and agreeing on three critical issues:

1. Your current job responsibilities
2. Responsibilities your boss has that you could be empowered to do
3. Future goals and objectives for you to pursue

Discussing and agreeing on these three issues will take some time; once completed, you will have the foundation for developing the process.

Clarifying Your Current Job Responsibilities

Ideally . . .

Initially both you and your boss should work through the following process together. Called the "A-B-C–1-2-3 Process," it is an easy way to help you update your current responsibilities and establish your priorities. Here is the procedure:

1. Don't waste your time pulling out your official job description. It's probably so old and outdated that it barely resembles what you currently do. Instead, make a list of everything you currently do. Call it "My Everything List."

My Everything List

1. _____
2. _____
3. _____
   _____
   _____
   _____
   _____
   _____
   _____

2. Divide your Everything List into A, B, and C columns. Column A represents your "Gotta Do" list; column B, your "Should Do?" list: column C your "Nice to Do" list.

My Everything List Divided

A. Gotta Do	B. Should Do?	C. Nice to Do
_____	_____	_____
_____	_____	_____
_____	_____	_____
_____	_____	_____
_____	_____	_____
_____	_____	_____

A List Prioritized

A. Gotta Do

1. _____

2. _____

3. _____

4. _____

5. _____

3. With your boss, make decisions on column B ("Should Do?"). Each item must become either a Gotta Do (column A), or a Nice to Do (column C). So much for column B. It's gone.

No Column B

B. Should Do?
(Gone.)

Column C Filed Away

C. Nice to Do
(Also gone.)

4. Column C, Nice to Do, needs to be filed away or temporarily set aside. Its contents don't represent critical responsibilities of your job. Be-sides, if an item in the list eventually becomes important, you'll probably know about it in advance and know where to find it.
5. You're now finished with the A-B-C part of the process. Next, take your A list and determine your priorities, with 1 being the most important, 2 the second most important, and so on. If possible, indicate the approximate amount of time each item requires. It may also help if your boss blesses your list.

You should now have a realistic and updated list of your primary job responsibilities and a handle on the amount of time these tasks take. Of course, your list is subject to change, but that's okay; today, change is constant.

Responsibilities Your Boss Could Empower You to Do

The next area to consider in developing your partnership looks at responsibilities your boss currently has that he or she could em-power you to do. Empowerment is stage 4 of the partnership model and is today's version of what used to be called delegation. The term has changed, but the principles remain the same.

Too often, bosses are guilty of insufficient empowerment, think-ing they have to do everything themselves. The result is a con-tinuing increase in their responsibilities, with no end in sight.

Is your boss guilty of this? There are some signs both of you can examine.

How to Tell When Your Boss Is Taking On Too Much

- Your boss is constantly taking work home.
- Your boss is always working overtime.
- When he or she is away for more than a day, important work doesn't get done.
- There are too many aspects of the work that only your boss knows.
- There are few decisions you can make on your own.
- Your boss micromanages employees, including you.

If these characteristics sound familiar, the verdict is . . . *Guilty!* You now have a prime candidate for the empowerment process.

To assist in determining what you could be empowered to do, have him or her make a list of current job responsibilities just as you did when you were clarifying your own critical tasks. He or she can then study the items and check those that could be delegated to you.

Here are some characteristics your boss can consider when determining what tasks you could be empowered to do:

- Tasks that are routine and ongoing—for example, weekly or monthly reports or other items that are well established
- Tasks that have an established procedure or a clearly defined outcome
- Tasks that will enable you to develop further professionally

Of course, there are certain job responsibilities your boss should not empower you to do—for example:

- Tasks involving highly confidential information
- Tasks that involve settling conflicts among other employees
- Tasks that are not clearly defined

The Empowerment Process

How the empowerment process is established is absolutely critical to your success. The most common mistake bosses and employees make in this process is failure to spend enough time discussing mutual expectations. Theoretically, your boss should know the empowerment process and how to establish it with you. But since we deal in reality, use the following points to ensure clear expectations:

- **Have a clear picture of the end result.** Your boss *must* have a clear picture in his or her mind of what the final result should look like. If you hear him or her making statements such as "You know what I mean" or "You'll figure it out," be very careful. Your boss doesn't have a clear picture of the end result, and you can't possibly produce an expected result when you don't know what that result should look like.

- **Ask questions to clarify expectations.** Throughout the clarification process, be sure to do the following: ask questions, ask questions, ask questions. Don't become overbearing, but be sure you understand precisely what you are expected to do when your boss is delegating a task to you.

- **Agree to what "acceptable performance" means.** Too often when a boss delegates to an employee, the expectation is that the assignment will be done exactly the way the boss would do it. This isn't realistic. You and your boss need to establish at least two levels of performance expectations:

    1. *"Acceptable performance" level.* This level indicates the expected result considering you're new to the task. It can be measured by time, dollars spent, dollars saved, per-

centages, quality, quantity, or something else. It's important that you and your boss establish this level in the beginning so you can track your progress.

2. *"Above-acceptable" or "good" performance level.* You should also establish an "above-acceptable" performance level. This indicates you've exceeded expectations, by whatever measurements you and your boss have established. It will be very useful when performance appraisal time comes.

Of course, by determining acceptable and above-acceptable performance levels, you automatically establish a below-acceptable level. Although the thought of this outcome isn't exactly pleasant, it sometimes happens. More important, once you and your boss have determined these levels, you have the measurements by which you can determine your own success.

Following is a model that may help you to determine these levels of performance:

- **Establish a time line with checkpoints.** Has your boss ever given you an assignment and said, "Come see me if you have any problems"? Certainly the intention is to give help when help is needed, but too often things get away from us.

  A way to prevent this from happening is for you and your boss to determine a time line for extended projects. This establishes a beginning date, ending date, and checkpoints in between when the two of you will sit down to see how things are going. A visual example of a time line model follows:

  Think of the time line as a goal with objectives. The goal should have a beginning date (BD) and a due date (DD).

Empowerment Performance Model

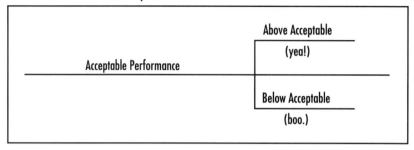

The objectives (O) are checkpoints with dates (D) in be-tween when specific tasks should be accomplished. These points also represent dates when you should be meeting with your boss to discuss your progress on the project. When the objectives are completed, the goal is accom-plished.

When determining the time line, answer four questions:

    1. When is the goal or task due?
    2. When should it begin?
    3. How many checkpoints need to be established?
    4. What objectives need to be accomplished by each checkpoint?

Plot the task, checkpoints, dates, and objectives in writing using the following model:

Time Line Model

Beginning Date Objectives	D	D	D	D	D	Due Date Goal
	O	O	O	O	O	

Plotting a Time Line

Project: _____

Due Date: _____ Beginning Date: _____

Checkpoint 1 _____ Date: _____

Objective: _____

_____

_____

Checkpoint 2 _____ Date: _____

Objective: _____

_____

Checkpoint 3 _____ Date: _____

Objective: _____

_____

Project Due: Date: _____

The number of checkpoints and objectives will vary according to the goal or project you're working on, but the point is to establish and plot any project of significant length that your boss empowers you to do.

- **Clarifying your limits of authority.** When your boss empowers or delegates a task to you, you typically know what your responsibility is. But too often there is no discussion about how much authority you have to carry out your responsibility. This can easily result in misunderstandings and other problems.

  How much authority you have is usually represented by expenses you can sign for or decisions you can make.

  Will this task require expenditures? If so, you both need to estimate a total and intermediate limits you would have the authority to sign.

  The issue of decisions is a biggie. It is usually the area where misunderstandings most commonly occur. What decisions can you make on your own? Which should you bring to your boss? If your boss doesn't make this clear to you, ask questions, so you're clear on what your decision authority is or isn't.

  From your boss's point of view, decisions can fall into three types:

  1. *"Do it. I don't need to know."* These represent areas where you have complete freedom to act as you think you should without consulting with your boss.

  2. *"Do it, and tell me about it."* This is your call. Nevertheless, these decisions represent judgments you've made that your boss needs to be aware of. There's no need for unnecessary surprises.

  3. *"Tell me first. Then we'll decide."* These are issues

you need to discuss with your boss *before* you act. They represent borderline situations you may encounter that may be beyond your authority. Better to be safe now than sorry later.

Obviously, you can't put all situations into these three categories, but the better you and your boss can plan the decisions you may have to make, the fewer problems you will both encounter.

- **Remove or take care of potential obstacles in advance.** Obstacles are problems your boss could easily take care of, but if left unattended can cause you great pain. Often this simply means letting others know you've been placed in charge of a particular project and what authority you have.

- **Evaluate the outcome.** Once you've completed the project or task, it's time to have a chat with your boss to discuss the quality of the end result. If acceptable and above-acceptable performance levels were established, you should already know how well you did, but a discussion helps bring closure to the project.

Your boss should be the one to take the initiative on this, but as you know, bosses tend to get busy and forget things, so it may be up to you to ask for the evaluation.

Using the empowerment performance model, you can focus on the following:

1. *Acceptable performance:* If the evaluation meets the expected performance levels, discuss the successes, and identify any specific adjustments you could make the next time.

2. *Above-acceptable performance:* If the evaluation is above the expected performance level, discuss the suc-

cesses, celebrate the outcome, and identify any minor adjustments that you might make in the future.

3. *Below-acceptable performance:* If the evaluation falls below the expected performance level, there's a problem. Usually this indicates unclear or unrealistic expectations from the beginning or failure to honor the time line. You and your boss need to identify the issues and make adjustments to prevent this from occurring again.

Evaluating the outcome is a critical step in the empowerment process. If the task has been successful, good; if it exceeded expectations, great. If the end result fell below expectations, it's *especially important* to identify what could be done differently next time.

Case Study

Janet's boss is the vice president of administration for an oil company. Within the past year, there has been an unusual amount of turnover in the industrial relations department, and her boss has been asked to look into the situation.

He wants Janet to help him to gather the information for a report the president has asked him to compile. He mentions to her that she will need to visit with the human resources director to get the files on employees who either have been terminated or resigned within the past year.

When she visits with the director with the request, she is turned down because of the confidential nature of the files. In fact, the director angrily asks her, "Who do you think you are, asking for that kind of information?"

When she reports back to her boss, he calmly replies, "Don't worry about it, I'll give her a call and straighten things out." He does, and Janet gets the information needed for the report, but the director of human resources now has a negative impression of Janet.

What's the Moral of the Story?

The negative impression could have been avoided by a simple phone call. When your boss empowers you with an assignment, be sure he or she takes care of or removes the potential obstacles in advance—especially the people ones.

Bosses sometimes think that because they've put you in charge, others will respond to you the same way they would respond to them. They won't.

How to Avoid Potential Obstacles

- Discuss the issues with your boss.
- Determine where potential obstacles may exist.
- Ask your boss to inform others so they know you've been given the authority to complete the project. This is especially important if you will be interacting with others higher than you in the organization.

Can There Be Too Much of a Good Thing?

Once you and your boss experience multiple successes with empowerment, there may be a tendency to keep delegating additional tasks to you. Don't allow yourself to become overloaded with more than you can successfully handle. There are two things you can do to prevent this from happening:

1. Together, reprioritize your tasks so you both know what's most important.
2. Consider the possibility of delegating lesser important tasks to someone else. After all, you know the process now.

Empowerment or delegation is a wonderful concept. It gives your boss more time to do other things while enabling you to grow professionally. But it's a process that must be handled carefully so both of you can experience success.

Determining Future Goals and Objectives

The final step in laying the foundation for your partnership is to determine future goals and objectives for you to pursue. These should come from both your boss and you.

Higher management may delegate tasks to your boss in helping to meet higher organizational goals. You may then be empowered to assist in accomplishing these projects.

Additionally, you might determine certain goals for your professional development. Some of these can be personal, such as taking continuing education or college courses, while others will be directly related to your job responsibilities. In some cases, you need your boss's approval.

Goals and the Rubber Band Theory

The Rubber Band Theory refers to two types of individuals: those who don't stretch themselves at all and those who stretch themselves too much. You don't want to be in either category. A good performance goal should stretch your ability to achieve, but it also needs to be realistic.

You can use the acronym SMART to determine the validity of any goal:

S **Specific:** Is the end result specific? Can it be stated clearly?

M **Measurable:** Is the goal measurable (in terms of dollars quality, quantity, percentages, time, etc.)?

A **Achievable:** Is the end result achievable? That is, will it stretch you yet still be attainable?

R **Realistic:** Is the goal realistic under current conditions?

T **Timely:** Is this the right time? Where will it be on your priority list? Will it change your priorities?

Following is an example of a poorly stated goal and the new and improved version. The differences are obvious.

A Poorly Stated Goal

> Present an employee morale report to the senior vice president of administration.

The Much Improved Version

> Present an employee morale report to the senior vice president of administration by (date). The report will focus on employees' responses to the following:
>
> • The success of the new health and wellness program.
> • Responses to the modified flextime policy.
> • Reactions to the new medical insurance guidelines.

As you can tell, the second version contains elements from the SMART acronym for stating goals. A specific due date is included along with the particulars of the report.

Determining Objectives

As in the empowerment process, any good goal must have checkpoints and objectives to help ensure success completion.

Following is an example of what the goal and its objectives might look like for the employee morale report:

Once you've finished the checkpoints and objectives, you can put the information on a time line to complete the initial process.

Goal

(Date) Present an Employee Morale report to the Senior Vice President of Administration. The report will focus on employees' responses to the following:

• The success of the new health and wellness program

• Responses to the modified flextime policy.

• Reactions to the new medical insurance guidelines

Objectives:

Checkpoint 1   Date: _____

Objective: Complete Survey Design

Checkpoint 2   Date: _____

Objective: Distribute Survey

Checkpoint 3   Date: _____

Objective: Complete Survey Collection

Report Due: Date: _____

What If Conditions Change?

Unfortunately, stuff happens. When you establish your goals and objective, you're doing so under existing conditions. If conditions change during the process of completing a goal, you and your boss need to discuss the changes and modify the goal so you're not accountable for something you can't control.

Summary

If you want to develop a working partnership with your boss, both of you have to take some time to lay a good foundation. This means clarifying your current job responsibilities, determining what your boss can empower you to do, and determining future goals and objectives. Here, in summary, is the process:

To Clarify Your Job Responsibilities:
The A-B-C–1-2-3 Process

1. Make a list of everything you do.
2. Divide your list into three columns: Gotta Do (A), Should Do (B), and Nice to Do.
3. Get rid of column B. Determine which items should be in column A (Gotta Do) or column C (Nice to Do).
4. File column C (Nice to Do) away somewhere. It will be there if you need it.
5. Prioritize column A (Gotta Do).
6. Have your boss bless your list (*optional*).

To Be Empowered With Other Responsibilities

1. Have a clear picture of the end result.
2. Ask questions to clarify expectations.

3. Agree to what acceptable and above-acceptable performance means.
4. Establish a time line with checkpoints.
5. Clarify your limits of authority.
6. Remove or take care of potential obstacles in advance.
7. Jointly evaluate the outcome.

To Determine Future Goals and Objectives
The SMART Acronym

S **Specific:** Is the end result specific?

M **Measurable:** Is it measurable? How?

A **Achievable:** Is the goal achievable?

R **Realistic:** Is it realistic under current conditions?

T **Timely:** Is this the right time to take on a new goal?

4

Problem Solving and Decision Making

As you are developing your partnership with your boss, you will probably be called on to act in his or her behalf. Sometimes you will have to make good decisions in various situations—team settings, one-on-one meetings with other department personnel, external customers, and so on.

Some situations are simple and straightforward, requiring little thought or analysis to reach a conclusion. Others aren't that simple, and may require careful analysis before you make the appropriate decision.

Following is a seven-step process for problem solving and decision making for the situations that aren't so easy. Included are a number of questions that will help you focus on the issues. You can choose the ones that apply to your particular situation.

"I've Got a Problem . . . What to Do?"

• **State the "apparent" problem.** There may be more to the situation than meets the eye. But the first thing you need to do is to determine what you *think* the problem is.

Questions to Ask

1. What is happening that shouldn't be?
2. What isn't happening that should be?

• **Analyze the situation.** There are two areas to watch out for in this step, which is the most important one in this process:

1. *"Shooting from the hip."* Sometimes in your zest to solve the apparent problem, you may not spend enough time fully examining the issues surrounding the situation. This almost always results in a poor decision.
2. *"Paralysis analysis."* At other times you may want to be so certain of making the right decision, you keep gathering information, fearing you can never have enough. This results in delay and may cause others to question your ability to reach timely conclusions.

When you finish analyzing the situation, you may discover that what you thought was the problem is only a portion of it, or that you have a different problem altogether. Therefore, there are many questions you might ask in this step.

Questions to Ask

1. Why did this happen?
2. Who or what is involved?
3. Who or what is affected?
4. When or where did this occur?
5. Is there supporting evidence?
6. What is the severity of the situation?
7. Is it a unique or recurring problem?
8. Do we have a policy to address the issue?
9. Whose opinions would be helpful?
10. Has this happened before?
11. What other questions would my boss ask?

• **Restate the problem if necessary.** After the analysis, you may realize that what you thought was the problem isn't, or that a more clearly defined situation exists. If this is the case, restate the problem as specifically as possible.

Questions to Ask

1. Is the original apparent problem still accurate?
2. If not, what are the related issues?
3. What new issues have been discovered that need attention?

• **Develop possible solutions.** It's time to brainstorm—the creative, imaginative stage of the process. Here you develop as many solutions as possible, including those that may even seem absurd at first. The key is to generate ideas at this point, *not* to evaluate them.

Questions to Ask

1. What are the possible alternatives for a solution?
2. What new approaches might be considered?
3. Do we have an existing policy to address the issue?
4. Whose opinions would be helpful?
5. Should I get my boss's ideas?

• **Project the results of each possible solution.** After you've determined possible solutions, it's important to play the "What if?" game with each of the possible alternatives to help you determine the probable result of your final selection.

Questions to Ask

1. What are the risks of each solution versus the expected gains or benefits?
2. Will the solution set a precedence for similar future situations?

3. Which solution will give the greatest results with the least effort?
4. Which solution meets the personal and professional preferences of others involved?
5. Are there other departments, such as Human Resources or Legal, that need to be involved in the selection?
6. Whose opinions might be helpful in projecting the results?
7. Will the results of the solution need to be measured? If so, how?
8. Should I consult with my boss at this point?

• **Select the solution and implement it with a time line.** The time line can be very useful here. Not all problems will require a solution with a time line, but some do. The others will at least need implementation and completion dates.

Questions to Ask

1. Does the solution require a time line?
2. How should the checkpoints be sequenced?
3. Who else should be involved in the implementation?
4. Does my boss need to be informed at this point?

• **Evaluate the results after implementation.** If you used a time line, evaluate the results at each checkpoint and at the end of the time period. If you do not use a time line, review your final decision after an appropriate amount of time.

Questions to Ask

1. How successful was the final decision?
2. Did it go as planned?
3. Is there anything else that should have been considered?

4. Were there any unexpected negative results?
5. How did those affected react to the final solution?
6. What could be done differently next time?
7. Should I discuss the results with my boss?

Summary

There will be many times in your partnership when you will be called on to analyze problems and make decisions on your boss's behalf. To help you focus on the issue, follow these guidelines:

Problem-Solving and Decision-Making Guidelines

1. State the "apparent" problem.
2. Analyze the situation. (This is the biggie.)
3. Restate the problem if necessary.
4. Develop possible solutions.
5. Project the results of each possible solution.
6. Select the solution and implement it with a time line.

5

Persuading and Influencing Your Boss

"So I Have This Wonderful Idea . . ."

So you do. Now all you have to do is convince your boss that it's a wonderful idea.

Trying to persuade and influence your boss may sometimes be a difficult task, and too often you might add to the difficulty yourself by using the wrong approach. You may have an idea that you think is good, and of course you might assume your boss will think the same way (*not* a good assumption).

Consequently, your approach can often become self-centered, leaving out the benefits to the organization and your boss's needs. As a result, you may face resistance to your proposal.

To be successful, you have to develop an approach that not only meets your needs, but also the needs of the person you're trying to convince—in this case, your boss.

Think of persuading and influencing as a negotiation process. In successful negotiations, everybody wins. The basic objective is to integrate as much as possible the needs, interests, and objectives of both parties. In attempting to sell your boss on an idea, you will be most successful when he or she is convinced of the merits of your proposal. This is best accomplished by being able to answer two key questions in advance:

1. How will the organization benefit?
2. How will my boss benefit?

Of course, you already know how *you* will benefit from your idea, but if you can clearly define the benefits to the organization and to your boss, you will greatly increase the chances of getting your idea blessed by your boss.

"How Do I Sell My Wonderful Idea?"

The following seven steps will help you convince your boss of the merits of your idea.

Step 1: Prepare for the Discussion

Don't you just love homework? Well, love it or not, it's the first—and most important—step in selling your idea. Too often people try to convince others of their point of view without sufficient preparation. Considering the following issues before your discussion will greatly boost your chances of success:

• **Objective.** Define what it is you want to accomplish. In other words, what do you want your boss to do as a result of the proposal?

• **Benefits to the organization.** Clearly identify how your proposal will benefit the organization. Will it save money or time, increase efficiency, or something else?

• **Meeting your boss's needs.** Identify how your boss will benefit from your idea. What's in it for him or her? Professionally? Personally?

• **Objections.** Put yourself in your boss's position. What objections might he or she have? How can you answer these objections if they occur?

- **Timing.** Timing consists of two issues: how much time you need to cover the subject and whether this is the appropriate time to present your concept in the first place. Will your proposal conflict with other tasks already in process? Might it be better to present your idea later?

- **Alternatives.** Try not to go for all or nothing at all. If your boss rejects your proposal or parts of it, what other alternatives might there be? Where can you compromise and still satisfy your needs, the needs of the organization, and your boss's needs?

- **Format.** Determine the order of your presentation. It should have a clear introduction, body, and conclusion. Consider visuals. Would charts or graphs help present clarify your ideas or benefits?

Step 2: Present Your Ideas

After you've done your homework it's time to present your proposal to your boss. Explain your proposal, clearly identifying the objective and how it will benefit both the organization and your boss.

If your boss is particularly knowledgeable about the subject, it may be helpful to identify some of the problems that may be encountered and how they can be overcome. By your giving both the pros and cons, your boss will know that you've done a thorough job in analyzing the situation.

Step 3: Ask Your Boss for a Reaction

Depending on your boss's communication style, this may or may not be necessary. But if your boss isn't responding, either positively or negatively, ask for feedback.

Step 4: Ask Questions and Listen Carefully

If you are going to understand your boss's reaction to your idea, you must do more than merely accept the first reaction you get. If your boss has concerns, listen carefully. Don't argue. Instead, ask why he or she feels that way and perhaps respond later to the objections.

Step 5: Identify Areas of Common Agreement

Just as it is important to deal with possible objections, it is also necessary to confirm the areas where you and your boss agree so you can continue building on your idea.

Step 6: Develop Alternatives

After you've identified where you and your boss agree, define the areas where some differences still exist, and together identify alternative solutions. The key is to provide the opportunity to explore possible options that may satisfy any previous concerns.

Step 7: Determine an Action Plan With a Time Line

Once your proposal has been modified and accepted, it's time to set your goal with its objectives and dated checkpoints. You can use the time line model to organize the process.

• • • • •

It might also be a good idea at this point to clarify your responsibility and degree of authority. (But you already know how to do that.)

QUESTIONNAIRE
How I Influence My Boss

Below are nine situations you might encounter when trying to influence your boss. While there are no *absolute* correct answers,
circle the one you believe is the most effective way to handle
each situation. The suggested answers follow the questions.

1. **When I've made a recommendation to my boss and there is
   no reaction at all, I should:**

   a. Ask, "Would you like to think it over for a while?"
   b. Ask, "What questions or comments do you have?"
   c. Repeat the benefits and key points of my idea.

2. **When my boss expresses an idea or point of view that runs
   counter to mine, I should:**

   a. Critically review the objection in an attempt to eliminate
      it.
   b. Ask my boss to elaborate the reasons for opposing the idea.
   c. Attempt to direct my boss's attention away from the objec-
      tion rather than comment on it.

3. **When I've finished outlining a proposal to my boss, I
   should:**

   a. Ask, "What are your reactions to my proposal?"
   b. Sum up the major advantages and key points in my idea.
   c. Ask, "Do you have any questions?"

4. **When my boss has objected to a portion of my recommendation and I've answered the objection, I should:**

   a. Say, "Okay, I'll move ahead on it then."
   b. Ask, "Are there any other points that you would like to
      discuss?"
   c. Remain silent to see what other objections there might be.

5. When my boss agrees with my proposal I should:

a. Say, "Thank you," and leave as soon as I can.

b. Express appreciation for the support.

c. Determine, with my boss, what action steps should be taken next.

6. When I've completed my presentation and my boss says, "Your proposal sounds pretty good, but I think you've missed some critical points," I should:

a. Keep quiet to see what else he or she may have to say.

b. Try to overcome the statement by presenting additional data and facts supporting my proposal.

c. Ask, "Could you give me a reason that you feel that way?"

7. When my boss accepts parts of my proposal but rejects other portions of it despite my attempt to sell the whole thing, I should:

a. Keep pushing for acceptance of the whole proposal since I've already sold part of it.

b. Give up for now, clarify what we seem to agree on, and try to negotiate the remaining portions on which we disagree later.

c. Give up and come back later with a completely revised proposal since total acceptance on the original idea is highly unlikely.

8. When I've made a recommendation to my boss and the response is, "That's an interesting idea, but I'd like to think about it," I should:

a. Say, "Okay, I'll talk to you about it at another time."

b. Ask if there are any other parts of the proposal that needs further clarification.

c. Summarize some of the benefits that may be lost if action on the recommendation is delayed.

9. When trying to influence my boss, I should:

a. Try to express myself in a persuasive manner.

b. Identify how my idea will benefit the organization and meet my boss's needs.

c. Focus on developing a well-prepared, detailed proposal.

Suggested Answers

Following are suggested answers to the questionnaire. Although there may be exceptions based on your boss's communication style, these are generally considered the most appropriate.

1. b: Ask, "What questions or comments do you have?" If your boss doesn't react at all, it is important to draw out his or her opinions to determine at least the initial reaction to your idea.

2. b: Ask my boss to elaborate the reasons for opposing the idea. It's important to find out why there is opposition to what you're proposing. The best thing for you to do in this case is to listen carefully in order to understand your boss's point of view.

3. a: Ask, "What are your reactions to my proposal?" Hopefully your boss will give you a reaction without having to ask for it, but if not, it's appropriate to ask for an initial response.

4. b: Ask, "Are there any other points that you would like to discuss?" It may seem that this is a good time to leave well enough alone. It isn't. It's better for you to discover if there are other concerns your boss may have rather than assuming everything else is fine.

5. c: Determine, with my boss, what action steps should be taken next. Congratulations! If your boss accepts your proposal, the next step is to determine the time line, checkpoint dates, and objectives to get things rolling.

6. c: Ask, "Could you give me a reason that you feel that way?" Although you may have done your homework, it's possible you may have missed some important points. Here, it's appropriate to draw out your boss's opinions without getting defensive. Focus on listening so you can respond later to your boss's concerns.

7. b: Give up for now, clarify what we seem to agree on, and try to negotiate the remaining portions on which we disagree later. It's important to know when to let go. Remember that when presenting a proposal, you can't always expect to walk away with everything you want. Perhaps you can come back later to negotiate the other areas, or perhaps you and your boss can develop other alternatives to deal with the objections.

8. a: Say, "Okay, I'll talk to you about it at another time." Sometimes it isn't good to push things. Maybe your boss is concerned about other issues, or maybe this just isn't the right time. It may be better to bring your proposal up later when your boss might be more receptive to your idea.

9. b: Identify how my idea will benefit the organization and meet my boss's needs. While a detailed proposal may be important, defining the value of your proposal to the organization and to your boss's concerns are primary to having your idea accepted.

Summary

Presenting proposals is a key aspect in developing a working partnership. Additionally, meeting the needs of both the organization and your boss will help establish you as a valuable player. Of course, *how* you present your recommendations will determine how well they are accepted, so keep these steps in mind.

How to Sell Your Ideas to Your Boss

1. Prepare for the discussion. Consider:
   - The objective
   - Benefits to the organization
   - Meeting your boss's needs
   - Objections your boss may have
   - Whether this is the right time
   - What other alternatives might exist
   - What format would be the most effective
2. Present your ideas.
3. Ask for a reaction.
4. Ask questions and listen carefully.
5. Identify areas of common agreement.
6. Develop alternatives.
7. Determine an action plan with a time line.

6

Performance Reviews and the Business Partnership

Oh, joyous occasion! It's performance review time. Perhaps you'd rather have your wisdom teeth removed with a pair of pliers.

The annual performance review historically is a time of pain for both bosses and employees. Bosses usually don't want to do it; they may put it off as long as possible, and then do it poorly. Employees get nervous, wonder how much of a raise they're going to get, and on judgment day they are typically disappointed.

It doesn't have to be that way.

When done as a partnership, the performance review can be a mutually beneficial experience for both you and your boss. The key is to establish a method to the madness to avoid the madness.

A Method to the Madness

There are three areas for you and your boss to consider when establishing your partnership approach to the performance review.

Frequency of the Review

Traditionally, the performance review is given once a year (hence the name: *annual performance review*). However, once a year has its problems. How can your boss possibly remember what you've done all year? How can *you* possibly remember what you've done all year?

Ideally, you and your boss should discuss your performance four times during the year. The first three reviews are unofficial but informative, and the last one is official, with few, if any, surprises. It's a great way for both of you to stay on top of things. Even if your company policy calls for a once-a-year review, there's nothing to say that you can't have quarterly discussions to see how things are going.

Which Method to Use

There are three basic types of performance review (though many variations).

   1. **The one-way system.** You may have been a victim of this method in the past. The one-way system is the source of the negative image performance reviews have had. Here's how it usually happens: Your boss (who just wants to get it over with) calls you in (sometimes without warning) and gives you your review in relatively short order. You have little to no input, and even if you are given the opportunity to respond, the review is still final. It's not a final experience.

   2. **The two-way system.** Some years ago, someone got smart and changed the method of performance reviews to a more positive approach, the two-way system. Here, both you and your boss review your performance together, with your boss having the final decision. (After all, the boss is the boss.)

The major advantage is that both of you have equal input into your performance review. Even though your boss has the final word, it affords you your opinion and presents a positive approach to the experience. This is a perfect example of the partnership approach and has proved to be highly popular with both bosses and employees.

3. **The 360-degree feedback system.** This relatively new approach to performance reviews is catching on with many organizations. The assumption is that since you interact with many people on many levels, a true appraisal should be a combination of responses from a cross-section of those you affect: your boss (naturally), peers, team members, and internal and external customers, for example.

The 360-degree feedback system is complicated and takes a lot of time to gather accurate data; however, when done correctly, its value is difficult to deny because it gives you a total picture of your performance.

Perhaps the best approach for you and your boss to take when determining the best method for your performance review is the two-way method, for the following reasons:

1. It is far better than the one-way system.
2. If your organization currently uses the 360-degree feedback approach, the two-way system can easily be incorporated.

What Tools Do We Need?

It's best to conduct your performance review four times a year. Because it's difficult to have these discussions from memory alone, you and your boss need some tools to help you keep track of how you're doing. Three will help.

An Ongoing Activity File

This is a file that both you and your boss maintain to track your performance throughout the year. Consider the following model:

- When your performance is at **acceptable standards,** there is no need for you or your boss to do anything with the file.

- When your performance is at **below-acceptable** or **poor standards,** your boss documents the situation, places it in the activity file, and discusses the performance with you, including specifics on how you can improve. This is not a happy occasion.

- When your performance is at **good** to **excellent standards,** your boss documents the situation, places it in the file, and discusses the performance with you. This is a happy occasion.

Since this is an ongoing file, you and your boss have a record you can reflect on when having your quarterly discussions and the official review. In another words, you don't have to remember anything.

Following are some suggestions for keeping the activity file:

- For legal reasons, advise your boss to maintain a file on each of his or her employees.

• There should be nothing in the file you're unaware of. The idea here is open communication between you and your boss and no surprises during your quarterly discussions or your official performance review.

• You should have access to your file with your boss's permission. Better yet, why not ask your boss for a duplicate copy that you can maintain and refer to?

• As your boss for the right to recommend entries. After all, you may do something outstanding in his or her absence that you feel deserves credit. (Of course it isn't likely that you'd recommend an entry if you messed up.)

• At the end of the official performance review, you can purge the file with the exception of any comments on ongoing goals, objectives, or other assignments.

The activity file is not an official file. It's a way for you and your boss to maintain an ongoing record of your performance so neither of you has to remember what you've done or how well you've done it.

Previous Goals and Objectives

A second tool of use in the performance review are previous goals and objectives you and your boss have already established. Each goal should have at least three standards: acceptable, above acceptable, and below acceptable. The more specific each level of performance is stated, the easier it will be to determine the outcome of the performance review.

Your Current Job Responsibilities

Chapter 3 covered how to determine your primary job responsibilities. This gives you a third tool that you and your boss can use to measure your performance. However, since things change with time, it is a good idea to update your current responsibilities, at least at the time of the official review. Quarterly is be even better.

"So, How Do We Proceed?"

For the two-way system to work well, careful preparation by you and your boss is necessary. Here is the step-by-step process.

Preparing for the Review

You and your boss set an appointment for the review at least five working days in advance. You both have some homework to do: You both fill out a blank copy of the review form (in pencil, signifying you're both willing to change your minds during the discussion).

When filling out the form, you and your boss can refer to your activity file, previously set goals and objectives, and a list of your current job responsibilities.

The Meeting

Following are some helpful hints for you and your boss to follow when you meet to discuss the performance review. You can vary the steps to fit your own needs.

1. Since you're using the partnership approach, either of you may lead the discussion.
2. Discuss each item on the form with the rating each of you determined. Use the activity file to help explain your positions. Where there is disagreement, you can discuss the issue. Your boss should make the final decision.

3. Discuss and evaluate any previously set goals and objectives. Were the results acceptable, below acceptable, or above acceptable? Were the measurements valid?

4. Discuss your current job responsibilities, and get agreement on future priorities.

5. Discuss both your strengths and areas where you can improve your performance.

6. Together, determine new goals and objectives with specific standards of performance and time lines for the next review period.

Some Things to Watch Out For

Interestingly enough, the research suggests that bosses and employees tend to rate the reviews very similarly. In addition, when there is a difference, employees tend to rate themselves lower than their bosses rate them.

Here are some issues that may come up during the review process and suggested ways to handle them:

• **You and your boss differ by one ranking on an item.** For example, your performance review is based on a five-point system, with 1 being the lowest rating and 5 being the highest. On a particular item, you score yourself at 3, and your boss ranks you at 4. In a situation like this, it's best to discuss why each of you scored where you did, and let your boss make the final decision.

• **You and your boss differ widely on an item.** When this happens, it usually indicates that the expectations and standards were unclear from the beginning. It's important here to be sure that when future goals and objectives are established, the expectations for acceptable, below acceptable, and above acceptable are crystal clear to both of you.

• **Conditions have changed.** You and your boss set your previous goals, objectives, and time lines under conditions existing at that time. But things change. When this happens, both of you need to discuss the expectations and modify them to fit the changing conditions. This could mean anything from changing the due date to dropping the goal altogether. In any event, you shouldn't be held accountable for changing conditions over which you have little or no control.

Summary

Performance reviews don't have to feel like a trip to the dentist without laughing gas. When approached through partnership, they can be positive and enlightening and lead to your continuing professional development.

How to Approach Performance Reviews

1. Use the two-way system.
2. Maintain an ongoing activity file.
3. Clearly document goals, objectives, and expectations for performance.
4. Periodically update your primary job responsibilities.
5. Prepare for the review in advance.
6. Determine and follow a specific process for the discussion.
7. Discuss differences, and seek agreement wherever possible.
8. Hope and pray for a *really* big raise.

7

Maintaining Your Professional Image

As an executive secretary or administrative assistant, you have a position of high visibility. Depending on your boss's position within your organization, and as a partner, you may be representing your department, division, or even the organization itself. This isn't a responsibility to be taken lightly.

How others see you is critical in determining how effective you are in getting things done. If you have a positive image, the people you deal with will be willing to cooperate; otherwise, you've got a big problem.

Here's the question: *What is your image in the organization? Is it positive? negative? Does it depend on whom you ask?*

The good news is you have control over how others see you. The bad news is that if you're not sensitive to how you're seen by others, it can hurt you, your boss, the department, the division, or even your organization. Remember that your effective partnership with your boss depends on the image you present.

Identifying Your Professional Image

Your professional image is formed by your actions and interactions with others on a daily basis. There are three elements that continually come into play in determining how others see you:

1. **Intended image**—how you would like to be seen by others.
2. **Perceived image**—how others see you. It's very important to know your perceived image because how others see you will determine your success or failure in representing your boss and your organization.
3. **Image difference**—the gap that exists between your intended and perceived image. The greater the gap is, the less realistic your intended image will be; the less the gap, the more accurate your intended image is.

The diagram shows how intended image, perceived image, and image difference connect:

Professional Image Model

Intended Image	Image difference	Perceived image
(as seen by self)	*(intent is to close)*	*(as seen by others)*

Perceived images are formed quickly. If they are initially negative, it takes a lot of work to change the perception to what your original intention might have been. In other words, it can be difficult to close the existing gap between your intended and perceived image.

However, you do have total control over how others see you. It's a matter of looking at yourself honestly and deciding what action you need to take to close the gap. Sometimes it's not an easy task, but your future in your organization may depend on it.

Following is an exercise that will help you identify your professional image.

EXERCISE
Determining Your Professional Image

List the adjectives that describe how you would like to be seen in the Intended Image column. In the Perceived Image column, list adjectives that describe how you think others perceive you. How do you know? What information have you received? Finally, write down specific actions you can take to reduce the gap between your perceived and intended images.

Intended Image   **Perceived Image**

_____   _____

_____   _____

_____   _____

_____   _____

_____   _____

Actions you can take to reduce your image difference.

_____

_____

_____

_____

_____

Reducing the Image Difference

Everyone has an image difference—the difference between their perceived and intended images. The important issue is its size and your effort in reducing it. This gap is similar to a blind spot— information other people know about you that you may or may not realize.

"How can this be?" you may be thinking. How can others know information about me that I don't know?" There are two ways this can happen:

1. Others have seen certain behaviors in you but haven't told you. This isn't your fault; you can't be held responsible for information you're not aware of.

2. Others have seen certain behaviors in you and have tried to tell you, but you haven't listened. This *is* your fault: you *are* responsible for not listening.

Often when others try to give us information about our behavior, we become defensive rather than receptive. Unfortunately, the only way to reduce our blind spot and image difference is to open ourselves to others' opinions. This is risky, but there isn't any other way to do it.

Following are ten steps you can take to facilitate the process:

1. **Select one or two individuals you trust.** Don't ask someone who always agrees with you or always disagrees with you. Pick someone you *know* will tell you the truth—maybe your boss, one or two peers, or someone from another department.

2. **Tell them what you're trying to do.** Explain that you would like to make certain changes in your behavior.

3. **Ask for their help.** Since changing a behavior is not a short-term process, ask for their assistance for a given period of time. Four to six weeks is a good estimate.

4. **Identify specific areas you want to improve.** This is critical. You need to pinpoint the behaviors you're concerned about. For example, you wouldn't want to say, "I'm trying to change my behavior, so let me know if you see a difference." This is too general a statement. Instead, you might say, "I know I have a tendency to interrupt others, and I'm trying to work on it. Would you be willing to help?"

5. **Agree to specific dates and times.** Go back to the time line. What you don't want to do is ask them to let you know when they are noticing certain changes. This is *your* responsibility. Therefore, you need to establish checkpoint meetings over the four- to six-week period to discuss their observations.

6. **Ask for their observations.** The purpose of these meetings is to listen to their point of view regarding changes they may have noticed in your interactions with others.

7. **Don't argue.** This is *really* important. You've asked for their feedback. Don't argue, don't defend, and don't rationalize or explain why you may have acted a certain way. If you do, you'll be shooting the messenger you selected.

8. **Use negative assertion.** Negative assertion is a technique for accepting the truth about yourself. For example, during one of your meetings, let's say your confidant shares an observation with you. If you know there is truth in the statement, you simply agree to it by saying something like, "Yes, you're right. I am like that." Period. No argument, no defense, no rationalization. Your admission will enable you to see yourself as others see you and will aid you in reducing your image difference.

9. **Use negative inquiry.** Negative inquiry is a technique for uncovering reasons for others' viewpoints. If you don't understand what's being said, you can ask for specific examples. If they can give you the specifics and you see the truth in them, you're back to negative assertion. If they can't give you specific examples, try asking for a further explanation.

10. **Thank them.** This may be easier said than done, but remember, *you* asked for *their* help. For them to know you're sincere about your intent, they need to know you appreciate their help. Tell them so.

Not easy, right? If you're truly concerned about reducing your blind spot and image difference, you have to be willing to open yourself to this technique. Just be sure you choose one or two people you can really trust to be honest with you.

Giving and Receiving Criticism

How you give and receive criticism plays an important role in maintaining your professional image. If you do it appropriately, it enhances your role in your organization, including your partnership with your boss. If not, it can diminish your effectiveness tremendously.

How to Give It

Giving constructive criticism in a positive way can be difficult. It involves preparation, a helpful attitude, and an intent not to cause defensiveness on the part of the other person. Here are some guidelines that may help you when giving criticism.

Before Giving the Criticism

• **Be sure the feedback is timely.** Normally the best time to give criticism is as close as possible to the actual event; however, this is a judgment call and will depend on individual situations. Sometimes it may be better to wait for a more appropriate time.

• **Consider if the person can do anything about it.** It has been said that honesty is the best policy, but that's not necessarily true. For example, if you said to a man who was "follicly impaired," "Gee, I really don't like bald men," of what value is the criticism? Perhaps he could grow his hair long on one side and flap it over, wear a toupeé, spend a ton of money on a hair transplant, or even buy a hat. But in fact, the criticism is of little value because his state of baldness is probably not within his control.

• **Can you convey the information so that the individual will benefit and improve?** For someone to accept criticism positively, there needs to be an identified benefit. In other words, how will his or her situation be improved by accepting and responding to your criticism?

• **Select an appropriate environment.** You've heard it before: "Praise in public, criticize in private." But there's more to it than that. Sometimes you have to consider the physical setting itself. Perhaps your office area is best; perhaps his or her space is better; perhaps a neutral area is more appropriate. It's a judgment call, but something worth considering.

When Giving the Criticism

• **Be specific.** Don't speak in generalities. For example, saying to someone, "I really don't like your attitude," accomplishes nothing because the statement is too broad. Instead, indicate the specific behavior you're referring to, including particular examples of past situations.

• **Ask questions that will let you know if the other person understands your intended meaning.** Giving criticism is not the time for misinterpretation. Rather than assuming your criticism is being received as intended, ask specific questions to verify your points are understood.

• **If you expect change, clearly state your expectations, and indicate your willingness to share in resolving the situation.** One of the ways others judge our sincerity is by our willingness to help in resolving certain issues. If you indicate your willingness to be part of the solution, you increase the odds of the criticisms being received with less defensiveness. You may not always be able to help personally or professionally, but it won't hurt to try.

• **Be sure the other person feels the situation has been fully discussed before ending the conversation.** There are always three sides to every story: yours, theirs, and the truth. Maybe you can't always get to the truth, but you can at least be willing to listen to the other person's point of view. Often this results in better understanding and communication between both of you.

Caution: Never criticize when you're angry. If you do, there's no way you will be able to approach the situation with positive intent. In fact, it's almost guaranteed that the end result will be disaster. You'll wind up attacking the person rather than dealing with the issue, resulting in more of a problem than you originally had. If you're angry at the individual, wait until you get a grip.

How to Take It

Learning how to accept feedback is just as important as knowing how to give it, but it's never easy.

When you receive criticism from others, you don't have the choice of who's the bearer of the bad news. Nonetheless, there are some things you can keep in mind that may make the criticism easier to take.

During the Criticism

• **Avoid becoming defensive.** Even though this may be your first response, it would be better for you to listen to the criticism and at least gain insight into the other person's point of view.

• **Ask for specifics that are relevant to the feedback.** This is the same as negative inquiry. Ask questions and for examples so you can get a complete understanding of the message.

• **If some change seems necessary, ask the speaker to assist you in developing solutions or alternatives.** Just as your offering to help with the solutions when you give criticism is indicative of your sincerity, the same applies when you're on the receiving end. Try asking, "What would you suggest?" to indicate your willingness to hear the criticism and seek advice on how to correct the behavior.

• **Summarize what both of you have said.** It's important to summarize before ending the conversation to be sure you're both on the same wavelength. The summary should include any actions you may have agreed to.

After the Criticism

• **Assess the feedback for relevance and value.** Ask yourself, "What information can I take from this that will be of value to me?" Even when you don't think the criticism is accurate or the person is sincere, sometimes there is information that will help you later.

• **Consider the source of the feedback as you consider its validity and value.** There are two things for you to think about when considering the source:

1. **Multiple behavioral response.** This represents similar feedback you've heard before from different people. For example, if over a period of time, different people have said to you, "You're such a perfectionist," there's probably some truth to it, and it may be something you should carefully look into. Multiple behavioral response is usually indicative of a particular behavior in your blind spot or image gap you may not be aware of but should be.

2. **Quality singular response.** This one may be a little more difficult to validate. You've gotten a particular criticism from one individual only. How do you decide if the criticism has merit? The answer is a question of trust. Do you trust the opinion of the person giving you the criticism? If so, consider the criticism valid; if not, at least consider if there's any objective information you can gain from the experience.

• **Consider the position of the person when deciding how to deal with the feedback.** If the criticism is from your boss or someone else above you in the organization, you *really* need to stop, look, and listen. How you respond to this level of criticism can affect your success later.

If you don't think the criticism is valid, explain your views, but be very careful. Although you don't want to take the blame for something you may not be responsible for, you also don't want to burn bridges in your defense.

Here's a difficult statement: *Sometimes it's just best to swallow things.* On the other hand, if you believe the feedback is valid, you can use negative assertion and ask the individual for ideas on how to remedy the situation.

• **Thank the person for the feedback.** Whether you feel the criticism is valid or not, thanking the individual for sharing the information with you indicates your willingness to listen and respond positively to another person's point of view.

You will encounter criticism. It's a natural part of interaction in the workplace. But that's not the issue. The issue is how you give and receive it that makes the difference.

Summary

How others perceive you is critical to developing a successful working partnership with your boss. If you're well respected and liked, you'll have a much easier time getting things done. Otherwise, you won't represent your boss, department, division, or organization very well.

Additionally, how you give and receive criticism is key to establishing and maintaining a positive professional image. To that end, here are some things to remember:

- Identify your intended and perceived images.
- Seek the help of someone you trust to help you reduce your image gap.
- Don't argue, defend, rationalize, or explain when you've asked for feedback.
- Be constructive when giving criticism. Follow the guidelines.
- *Never* criticize when you're angry.
- Understand that multiple behavioral response indicates you may have a blind spot you need to examine.
- Recognize that quality singular response may be just as valuable as multiple responses.
- If it's your boss or someone else above you in the organization who is giving you a particular criticism, stop, look, and listen—very, very carefully.

8

How Do You Come Across to Others?

Every day in every way, you are constantly communicating and sending out messages that will determine how others perceive you. Getting in touch with how you send these signals is critical to developing a solid partnership with your boss, working effectively with your peers, and defining your professional image in your organization.

Basics of Communication Dynamics

Here are some of the basics about communication dynamics for you to consider.

• **You cannot *not* communicate.** Whether you seek interaction or intentionally attempt to avoid it, you are always communicating with others. Sometimes the messages you send are positive, and at other times negative.

Generally, when you seek interaction with others, the odds are in your favor for positive results. When you attempt to avoid communication, the odds increase for others to perceive you negatively. Something as simple as whether you acknowledge someone you pass in the hallway can lay the foundation for others to perceive you as being friendly or having your nose in the air.

• **Communication is irreversible.** Have you recently communicated something to someone you wish you hadn't? If you have and it's bothering you, you can at least hold yourself accountable and apologize, a good communication skill in itself.

• **Communication is intentional and unintentional.** One of the purposes of communication is to have the receiver understand the message as you intended to send it. However, it is all too easy to communicate unintentional messages. When this happens, it is up to you to rectify the situation; if you don't, it will build barriers between yourself and others.

• **Communication is primary to defining relationships.** How well you communicate has a direct bearing on the quality of your relationships with others. When you both have positive intentions, chances are that the future relationship will be positive. If the intentions are negative on either side, the stage is set for an adversarial future.

• **How others perceive your communication skills may determine your potential for advancement.** (This one's a little scary.) Your expertise and the specific skills you possess are no longer the only qualifications you need for professional growth. The interpersonal skills you use in performing tasks and relating to others are as critical in representing your boss and your organization. There are also determining factors when you are working on a team or with members of other departments.

Primary Characteristics of Interpersonal Dynamics

There are three primary characteristics of interpersonal dynamics that determine how you come across to others: visual, vocal, and verbal components.

The Visual

There are five elements of visual communication:

Eye Contact

In this culture eye contact is expected when communicating. Its absence may be perceived as a lack of sincerity, disinterest, lack of concern for the other person, or other negative interpretations.

Here is an example: You're working hard at your desk. Your fingers are flying on the keyboard; your eyes are glued to the screen. Someone calls your name. You look up and briefly acknowledge the person's presence. But as you're being spoken to, you keep working away at your computer, periodically indicating to the individual that you're listening.

Sound familiar? While you may be perfectly capable of working on one thing while listening to someone else, that's *not* the way it comes across. Instead, you need to take your fingers *off* the keyboard, your eyes *off* the screen, *stop* what you're doing, and *look* at the person you're communicating with. That's the expectation, and there's little you can do to escape it if you want others to see you as an attentive communicator.

Facial Expression

As with eye contact, your facial expressions send messages about your willingness to communicate with others. Facial responses are a visual animation of how you are reacting to a message. If you've ever attempted to relate to someone who responded with a stony facial expression, you've experienced the difficulty in reading that person's reaction to what you were attempting to communicate.

And there's more to it than that. It's very easy to be so focused that you may innocently pass someone in the hallway without smiling or nodding. It doesn't sound like a major offense. After all, you were busy. However, you may have left a negative impression because there was no facial acknowledgment. In a position of high visibility, this can be costly, because people will talk.

What to do? If you try to smile all the time, others may get suspicious and wonder what you're up to. Besides, smiling all the time isn't realistic. But if a lack of responsive facial expression is part of the feedback you've been given, you can try more verbal responses when communicating. When you pass someone in the hallway, simply say, "Hello." It will automatically animate your facial expression, softening the focused look you may have had.

Body Language

Another critical way you send messages to others is through your body language. Most often, body language, along with eye contact and facial expression, reinforces the words we use, solidifying the message. At other times, these messages are delivered without verbals, and if you're not telling the truth, your body posture, facial expression, and eye contact will actually contradict what you're saying.

Most of the time people read body language subconsciously, unaware they are visually interpreting the relationship between the other person's words and actions. If your words and actions are in sync, your message will be seen as honest. If your verbals and visuals are not in support of each other, you may not be believed because of an apparent contradiction between the auditory component (what they hear) and the visual component (what they see). When faced with the choice of the auditory versus the visual message, people believe what they see your body language do rather than what they hear you say.

Object Language

Object language is defined by how you visually present yourself to others. Your dress, hairstyle, jewelry—even how you keep your office area—sends messages to others about you. How these messages are interpreted will vary according to others' perception of what is appropriate in certain situations.

For example, dressing informally on "casual Friday" would normally be appropriate, but if you have important clients visiting, dressing in a more business-like way would be the better choice. The typical guideline is to dress to the expectations of others.

Some professionals might argue that dress or other elements of object language aren't indicative of your abilities. This is not a good position to adopt. In fact, how others react to the way you present yourself may determine if you are given the opportunity to show what your abilities are in the first place.

Proximics

Proximics refers to the dynamics of spatial relationships between people. Personal comfort zones vary according to cultures. In the United States, it is approximately one and a half to two feet. This is considered to be the personal space or circular bubble that belongs to each individual.

Sometimes people invade each other's space. When this happens, most people feel intimidated and step back; others may consciously hold their ground; a few may even step forward in a psychological attempt to "push" the intruder away.

If you work with someone who invades your space regularly, you've probably tried sending nonverbal messages, hoping he or she would get the message. It probably didn't work. Sometimes the only solution is to tell the individual in a polite but firm way that you're not comfortable with anyone being that close to you. Using *anyone* helps take any negative tone out of the situation. (Of course, depending on who the individual is, you may welcome the closeness, but that's another story.)

How Important Are These Visual Elements?

Very important. In face-to-face communication, the visual elements carry the majority of the message. When auditory and visual messages contradict each other, it's the visuals that override: people believe what they see over what they hear.

Although the percentages vary according to the research, these five visual components account for approximately 55 to 60 percent of the impact of how you come across to others.

The Vocal

There are four characteristics of vocal communications.

Rate of Speech

The average person speaks at 125 to 150 words per minute, depending on the part of the country in which he or she was raised or currently lives. Sometimes this variance in rate of speech can lead to questionable, even negative, impressions. For example, people living in the Northeast tend to speak much faster than those living in the South. It's not improbable that Person A, a faster talker, perceives Person B, the slower talker, to be a slow thinker, while Person B (the slower talker) perceives Person A (the faster talker) to be a fast-buck artist.

Inflection

Inflection is the body language of the voice through which emphasis is placed on certain words, enabling your listener to know how you feel about your subject. Typically, voice inflection works with eye contact, facial expression, and body language. Depending on your delivery, style, your message can sound interesting or dull.

Perhaps you remember a teacher in whose class your greatest challenge was staying awake. The knowledge may have been there, but the delivery wasn't, and as a result the message fell flat.

Volume

Volume, too, may indicate your feelings. Normally, a loud voice is a signal of high intensity, a lower voice a signal of less intensity. But this isn't always the case. For example, some people lower their volume when they are angry or upset, yet increase the intensity of their feelings. At times, this can be very effective in getting a message across. However, this technique requires self-control and an ability to focus on the issues rather than the emotions.

Generally you should strive for an evenly modulated volume. If your volume is too low, hearing becomes difficult; too loud, and you may appear overly excited or intense.

Tone of Voice

You've heard it before: "It's not *what* you say, but *how* you say it." When combined, rate of speech, inflection, and volume produces tone of voice.

Tone indicates whether you are angry, sincere, sarcastic, happy, sad, and so forth. It is the tone of your voice that communicates your vocal messages to others.

Sometimes you may be unaware of the tonal message you're sending. Perhaps someone responds by telling you that he or she doesn't appreciate the way you're talking to him or her. When this happens, it's important to realize that your tone may prevent the message from getting through as intended.

What's the Impact of the Vocal Elements?

Like the visual elements, the vocal components of face-to-face communication weigh heavily in how you come across to others. The research suggests that vocals account for approximately 35 to 40 percent of the impact of your message. And if you are talking to someone over the phone, the vocals represent most of the message since the visual components are nonexistent.

The Verbal

The final area in how you send messages to others is verbal. It consists of one essential element: words.

Your choice of words initially determines how your communication is likely to come across to others. Words that are considerate of others are likely to help deliver a more sincere message as opposed to random words you might choose without concern for their possible impact.

What's the impact of verbal elements?

Word choice accounts for only 5 to 10 percent of the impact in face-to-face communication.

Three Other Communication Elements

There are three other elements in the communication process. They don't fit into any of the three previous categories, but they are nevertheless important in how others perceive you.

The Time Factor

Your response to time sends messages to others regarding your organizational skills, sense of urgency, and respect for others' time. Negative or positive perceptions are partially determined by how you respond to the concept of time.

For example, when you are on time with tasks and meetings, you are seen as well-organized, having an appropriate sense of urgency, and considerate of others' schedules. When the opposite is true, you may be seen as being unorganized, having a laissez-faire attitude regarding task accomplishment, and being inconsiderate of others' responsibilities and obligations.

Tactile Communication

Tactile communication refers to the sense of touch, probably the most effective of all forms of interpersonal communication.

Today, the caution in the workplace is, "Don't touch." There's simply too much room for misinterpretation. The only safe thing left is the handshake.

Historically, the genders have been taught different values regarding this custom. Many men, especially those raised in the South, were taught at a very early age to initiate a firm handshake with a male, but to wait for a woman to extend her hand first, and then shake it gently. Today this still leads to misunderstanding when a woman gets a "dead fish" as a greeting.

By comparison, women were taught much later about the handshake, and some were never taught at all. It's only in the last two decades that shaking hands has become a unisex custom in the workplace.

Today, the safest approach regardless of gender is to initiate a firm handshake with everyone. Other than that, don't touch, unless you're sure you know who you're dealing with.

E-Mail

E-mail has become part of the communication process and it affects how you come across to others. Consider the following questions:

- How many people do you communicate with through e-mail only?
- What is your perception of them?

If e-mail is the main source of relating to someone, it's also the determining factor in forming the impression you have of each other. Although its purpose is quick and informal communication, it needs to be treated as a critical factor in defining your image.

Following are some helpful hints for using e-mail:

- Use both uppercase and lowercase letters appropriately.
- Use proper sentence structure and punctuation.
- Avoid errors in spelling and grammar usage.
- Avoid symbolic language that only you understand.
- Use a "Hello" and "Good-bye" appropriate to your reader.
- *Never* send an angry message; it could backfire.
- Remember that your e-mail message is an electric image of yourself.

Image Questionnaire

Below are ten questions relating to your communication style. Answer each one *true* or *false*.

1. ___ I'm aware of always giving eye contact when speaking to others.

2. ___ I'm aware of my facial expressions during my interactions.

3. ___ I'm conscious of the body language I use when communicating with my boss or peers.

4. ___ I'm willing to change the way I dress to complement the situation, location, or people I'm involved with.

5. ___ I don't invade others' personal space.

6. ___ I'm aware that my tone of voice could cause someone to misinterpret my message.

7. ___ I'm aware that my choice of words could have a negative impact on others.

8. ___ I'm always on time when completing tasks and attending meetings when it's within my control.

9. ___ I'm aware of when and when not to appropriately touch others.

10. ___ I'm aware that e-mail projects my image to others.

Any questions you answered false indicate areas you might want to consider in improving how you come across to others.

Interpersonal Skills That Promote Success

Here are five other thoughts that will help you in your communication quest:

• Be aware how you send messages to others. The more you are aware of the visual, vocal, and verbal messages you send to others when you communicate, the greater your ability will be to have the message perceived the way it was intended.

• Be aware of how you receive messages from others. Exercising active listening and feedback skills is critical to developing an effective partnership with your boss and working relationships with others. By listening well and giving effective feedback, you tell others that they count, their thoughts are valid, and they are deserving of your time. (More about listening skills in the next chapter.)

• Develop the ability to motivate others. You might think that this is a management skill, but it also applies to peer relationships. When you work with others, it's important to strive toward higher levels of performance.

• Be willing to be part of a team effort. Maybe you don't like teams, but with the renewed efforts in team building, you need to be willing to work interdependently rather than independently of others. This means giving up a certain amount of individuality in exchange for team recognition. But teams are here to stay, so you might as well get used to them.

• Work on effectively presenting oral and written information. Don't you enjoy listening to a good presentation? Those you may be presenting to do also. Especially when you are representing your boss, there's nothing better than being well organized and knowledgeable, and responding confidently to questions.

Barriers to the Effective Use of Interpersonal Skills

You've read *what* to do. Finally, here are a few items for you to watch out for.

Differences in Values

When you see things differently from others, there is a natural tendency to think you're right and they're not. If you allow this reaction to go unchecked, you raise barriers that prevent you from seeing the validity in the other's point of view. You may also appear inflexible.

Working With Someone You Don't Like

It is inevitable that you will have to work with individuals you wouldn't want to have over for dinner. However, you don't have to like someone to work with that person effectively. The best thing for you to do is stay focused and by all means be cordial and professional. If you're not, it could come back to haunt you later.

Defensive Communication

This can happen especially when you're working with someone you'd prefer not to. When you are in a defensive posture, your interpersonal skills suffer. Rather than attempting to be objective, the tendency is to take things personally instead of staying focused on the task. Talking about the issues may help, but if the other person isn't willing, you'll have to work through the issue on your own.

Language Barriers

Language barriers have various causes, but one of the most common is professional jargon. People in the same or similar job can communicate much more effectively with each other than with those in different positions. The only way to overcome this barrier is to be aware of the differences and adjust your vocabulary to the other person's level of understanding.

Another form of language barrier may occur when others speak English as a second language. The more severe their accent is, the greater the difficulty is in understanding them. This is a sensitive situation.

Although few are willing to admit it, difficulty in understanding others' accents often promotes the idea that they don't know what they're talking about. Of course, this isn't true, but it's very easy for some people to make the assumption. If this happens, the best thing for you to say is, "I didn't understand what you said. Could you please repeat that?" You'll come away with the message, and the other person will feel more confident that the message was communicated.

Unawareness of the Impact of Your Communication Style

Is it possible that your personal style of communication creates barriers that prevent others from wanting to interact with you unless absolutely necessary? If this is the situation, you need to be willing to confront yourself through feedback from others and make adjustments where necessary. Your future success may depend on it.

Summary

Remember these important points regarding how you communicate with others:

- You cannot not communicate.
- Communication is irreversible.
- Communication is intentional and unintentional.
- Communication is primary to defining relationships.
- How others perceive your communication skills may determine your potential for advancement.

You deliver messages to others through the visual, vocal, and verbal aspects of communication. Whether you are actively involved or intentionally attempting to void interaction, others will judge you by the way you come across to them.

Visually you communicate through your eye contact, facial expression, body language, object language, and proximics, accounting for 55 to 60 percent of how you project yourself to others. Vocally, you deliver messages through your rate of speech, inflection, volume, and tone of voice, accounting for 35 to 40 percent of your impact. Verbally, your words account for only 5 to 10 percent of your communication style.

Additionally, you send messages through your sense of timeliness and how you deal with tactile communication.

Others will also judge you by the image you present when using e-mail.

There are five specific skills that can help promote success with your boss and others:

- Being aware of how you send messages to others
- Being aware of how you receive messages from others
- Being able to motivate others
- Being willing to be part of a team effort
- Being able to present oral and written information effectively

Finally, there are five barriers that can hinder your effective Use of Interpersonal Skills

- Differences in values
- Not being able to adjust to working with someone you don't personally like
- Defensive communication
- Language barriers
- Being unaware of the impact of your communication style

9

Listening and Responding to Others

Do you think you're a good listener? If you're like most people, you probably think you are and unfortunately, you're probably not. Being a good listener doesn't just happen.

Critical to developing an effective partnership with your boss and working well with others is your ability to listen actively and respond. This doesn't mean simply nodding occasionally or saying "uh-huh" or "really" every now and then. It means using active listening and responding techniques that indicate you have clearly heard and understood the speaker. To do this requires skill and practice. The reward is enhanced communication.

Active listening and responding calls on both parties in the communication to work hard to create shared meaning. This means paying careful attention to both the content and feelings within a message—in other words, being in tune to the visual, vocal, and verbal cues you're receiving.

Actively responding is integral to good listening, and how you approach and give feedback to others is central to representing your boss accurately and being recognized as an effective communicator.

Sometimes the best way to respond to others in the workplace is with an effective question. Whether your interaction is with your boss, coworkers, or clients, asking good questions offers you the opportunity to tap into new information while showing both your concern and attention to the sender's message.

Hearing vs. Listening

"I heard you . . ." Yes, but were you listening? Hearing is simply the act of receiving audible sounds with the ear; it can leave your head buzzing but void of information. It's a physiological process requiring little or no concentration on your part and very little response to the speaker.

Listening, on the other hand, is active, requiring concentration, skill, and practice. Most people speak at an average rate of approximately 125 to 150 words per minute. However, you are able to process thought at four to six times that rate. This gives you a lot of free time to wander mentally. When this happens, you run the risk of missing the information unless you use specific tools to concentrate on both the message and the speaker.

Listening is not a natural activity in the communication process. It requires knowledge of listening skills, concentration on the speaker and the message, and continued practice. Perhaps most important, active listening requires a willingness to spend the time learning to become a better communicator.

Five Levels of Active Listening and Responding Skills

There are five levels of active listening and responding techniques. As you consider each level, determine which levels you currently use and which techniques you need to focus on to increase your listening effectiveness.

Level 1: Basic Acknowledgment

Basic acknowledgment is the simplest of the listening skills, yet very important in responding to the speaker's message. It encompasses both visual and verbal responses.

Visual acknowledgments include head nodding, leaning forward or backward, and crossing your arms or legs. Probably the most important visual acknowledgment others look for is the head nod, because it indicates you're paying attention to your speaker.

Verbal acknowledgments include responses such as "Uh-huh," "I see," "Really?" and "No kidding?"

A word of caution regarding basic acknowledgment: This method can be used to respond actively to others, but it can also be used *not* to listen. For example, you can take off on a mental vacation and simply check back in once in a while by saying, "Really?" or, "I see," or, "Uh-huh," without having listened to anything at all. You've done it before, and you'll probably do it again.

Level 2: Silence

Using silence as a listening skill may initially seem to be contradictory to responsiveness, but it isn't. Silence, or intentionally *not* saying anything when the speaker is at a natural pause in the conversation, encourages him or her to add information.

Silence can be overdone, or even used as a manipulation, but that would be contradictory to the original intent, which is to gain more information.

Level 3: Asking Questions

Asking questions tells the speaker two things: that you're interested in the message and want to know more. Questions are a powerful response tool for you to use in the active listening process. Following are some types of questions you can use in the active listening process:

• **Close-ended**—questions that can be answered with one or two words such as yes or no. *Example:* "Do you need this by Friday?"

• **Open-ended**—questions that encourage the speaker to give as extensive an answer as necessary. *Example:* "What do you think about this situation?"

• **Direct**—questions that ask for a very specific answer, usually limiting the response to the information requested. *Example:* "What procedure would you like me to follow?"

• **Probing**—questions designed to follow up another question and answer in order to solicit additional information. *Example:* "What else do you think should be discussed at the meeting?"

• **Hypothetical**—questions that represent a "what if—?" situation to which the speaker is asked to respond. *Example:* "What if I'm challenged on this issue? How do you think I should handle it?"

The Power of Questions

Questions are powerful tools of communication. They indicate initiative, a willingness to exchange information, and a desire to know more. When you ask good questions, you accomplish the following:

• You gain additional information.
• You stimulate further thought.

- You put yourself in temporary control of the situation.
- You imply you're interested in what someone has to say to you.

Level 4: Paraphrasing

Paraphrasing is a rather sophisticated listening technique that focuses on the content of the message. When you paraphrase, you put into your own words what you think the speaker is saying and then ask for confirmation. The best use of paraphrasing is to clarify a critical point or summarize a number of issues.

Guidelines for Paraphrasing

- Let your speaker finish his or her thought.
- In your own words, indicate what you *think* is being said. *Example:* "Let me see if I understand your position . . ."
- Ask for confirmation. *Example:* "Do I understand you correctly?"
- If your understanding is accurate, continue the discussion.
- If not, ask your speaker to give you more clarification. *Example:* "Can you explain this part a little more?"

Most people don't use paraphrasing very much. We're anxious to get our own opinion stated, without verifying the speaker's intent. But if you want to be perceived as a good listener, it's an excellent skill for you to develop.

On the other hand, you don't want to overuse this technique. For example, if someone casually says to you, "Hi, how are you?" don't respond by saying, "Gee, let me see if I understand what you mean by that . . ." It was just a greeting, and you went overboard.

Level 5: Reflective Listening

While paraphrasing focuses on content, reflective listening focuses on the emotion your speaker may be experiencing. For example, if you are listening to someone who seems frustrated or angry, you might address the emotion you think he or she is feeling by saying, "You really sound upset about this."

Reflective listening is a sophisticated listening skill. It tells the speaker that you're listening to both the content and the emotion he or she may be feeling yet not stating.

Use this technique carefully, because you run the risk of misidentifying what you think may be an underlying emotion. On the other hand, it certainly indicates your concern for the person sending the message.

Listening Questionnaire
Self-Assessment

Answer the following questions yes or no.

_____ 1. Are you generally interested in other people and what they have to say?

_____ 2. Even when you're listening to someone who initially bores you, can you find ways to get interested and stay with the conversation?

_____ 3. If a subject sounds difficult, are you willing to try to listen anyway rather than dismiss it?

_____ 4. Can you understand and appreciate views that are different from your own?

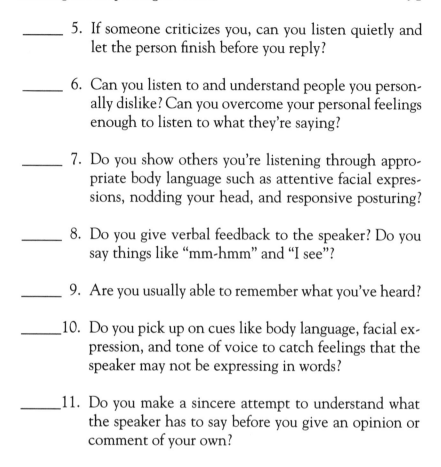

_____ 5. If someone criticizes you, can you listen quietly and let the person finish before you reply?

_____ 6. Can you listen to and understand people you personally dislike? Can you overcome your personal feelings enough to listen to what they're saying?

_____ 7. Do you show others you're listening through appropriate body language such as attentive facial expressions, nodding your head, and responsive posturing?

_____ 8. Do you give verbal feedback to the speaker? Do you say things like "mm-hmm" and "I see"?

_____ 9. Are you usually able to remember what you've heard?

_____10. Do you pick up on cues like body language, facial expression, and tone of voice to catch feelings that the speaker may not be expressing in words?

_____11. Do you make a sincere attempt to understand what the speaker has to say before you give an opinion or comment of your own?

Hopefully you were able to answer yes to all eleven statements; but you probably have a no or two scattered here and there. Following are some guidelines for you to consider to help you with your no responses.

Guidelines for "No" Responses to the Listening Questionnaire

1. Since you're probably busy most of the time, it's difficult always to be interested in others and what they may have to say. Certainly task accomplishment is critical, but so is the need for developing positive work relationships, especially your partner-

ship with your boss. One way to do this is to make time for others whenever you can, within reason. The more attentive you can be to others, the stronger your professional image will be.

2. When attempting to listen to someone who initially bores you, try asking specific questions to help move the conversation toward a conclusion. You can also try inserting leading statements such as: "So your concern is . . . ," "So you want me to . . . ," or "So your question is . . ." These kinds of statements help bring the speaker off tangents and focus on his or her specific point. This helps put you in control of the conversation and bring it to closure.

3. Just because a subject is difficult doesn't mean you shouldn't pay attention to it. You may want to ask yourself the following questions before dismissing the information:

- Could this issue help me in my professional development?
- Is the information critical to my job at this time?
- Will the subject become important to my job in the future?

4. Of course, you *think* you're right; however, there are other ways of viewing the same issue or solving the same problem. Not only is it important to listen to others' opinions, it is equally important to be able to accept, adjust, or compromise where you can. Having to be right all the time will quickly cause your coworkers to label you not only as being too opinionated, but also as being a poor listener.

5. This may be the most difficult question on the survey to answer yes to; however, it isn't impossible. In fact, you already have two methods you can use.

One is negative assertion. Is there truth to the criticism? If so, simply agree with the statement rather than defending yourself or rationalizing your actions. The other method is negative inquiry. If you're not sure there is truth in the criticism or you don't understand it, ask for examples or more information. Then use negative assertion if you agree with the information.

If you don't agree, simply say, "I disagree with your criticism," or, "I understand you see it that way," or a combination of both.

The key issues in using either of these techniques are to avoid getting defensive if the criticism is valid or being manipulated if it is intentionally unjust.

6. We tend to believe those we like and not believe those we don't. However, in business, liking someone is not paramount to measuring his or her truthfulness. Perhaps you don't like how he or she comes across to you, but beware of denying the validity of the message because of your personal feelings toward the messenger.

7. It's always important for you to maintain good eye contact, attentive facial expression, and responsive body language when listening to others. Anything less will be perceived as a lack of interest on your part by whomever you're communicating with.

8. "Mm-hmm" and "I see" are examples of Level 1 or basic acknowledgment listening skills. Use them frequently because they indicate your interest in what the speaker is saying.

9. Most people are not good listeners and tend to forget what others have said. If you practice using the five levels of listening skills described in this chapter, you will find yourself retaining more and more of what you've heard.

10. When you are practicing effective listening, pay close attention to changes in the speaker's body language, facial expression, and tone of voice. For example, a slight wrinkling of the forehead could be an indicator of momentary confusion.

Changes like these are sometimes significant and should be addressed when they occur in the conversation.

11. Too often, we are quick to respond with our opinion rather than making sure we are clear about what the speaker is saying. To verify the speaker's intent, use a combination of questioning techniques and paraphrasing before jumping in with your opinion.

Improving Listening and Responding Skills

Here are some guidelines for becoming a better listener:

- Prepare to listen.
- Choose the appropriate time and place when possible.
- Control or eliminate distractions whenever you can.
- See listening as an opportunity to learn more.
- Set aside a time to listen if the issue is very important.
- Monitor the way you listen. Focus on using the five levels of active listening skills and the visual, vocal, and verbal aspects of communication.
- Make your feedback prompt, accurate, concrete, and specific.
- React to the message, not the speaker.
- Concentrate on exchanging meaning.

Summary

Listening is not the natural process most people think it is. In fact, most of us are not so hot when it comes to using this skill. But being a good listener is a critical skill when establishing a partnership with your boss or working effectively with others.

Fortunately there are tools we can tap into to help increase our ability:

- Basic acknowledgment (both visual and verbal), which includes nodding your head and saying "uh-huh" or "I see"
- Silence, which encourages the speaker to add information
- Asking questions, which tells the speaker you're interested and want to know more
- Paraphrasing, which helps you to clarify what the speaker has said
- Reflection, which helps you to identify the emotion the speaker may be experiencing

The more you can develop your ability to listen, the more you will enhance your image as an outstanding communicator to your boss and others with whom you work.

10

Managing Conflict With Your Boss (and Others)

After all this stuff about developing a wonderful working partnership with your boss, how can conflict possibly occur? Because
it will.

One of the few things you can count on is that conflict will occur
in the workplace. What's important is how you handle it when it
happens. In fact, your ability to deal with conflicts effectively and
successfully may be one of the determining factors on your performance review, how well you participate in or lead teams, manage a project, or whether you're considered for a promotion. It is
vital to your partnership with your boss.

Characteristics of Conflict

Conflict is Inevitable

Because different people have different values, beliefs, and atti-
tudes, conflict will occur in relationships. Once you accept this as
a fact, you can focus on ways to manage it rather than pretend it
doesn't exist or always has to be avoided.

Conflict Can Be Productive or Destructive

The determining factor to this dynamic is the individuals involved in the situation. If both sides are willing to focus on the is-

sue, the result can be productive; if the focus is on attacking each other, the result will be negative and will contribute to the deterioration of the relationship.

Not All Conflicts Will Be Resolved, But Most Can Be Managed

True conflict resolution is very difficult to achieve; however, there are at least five methods of managing conflict you can use depending on the situation and the individuals involved (more about this shortly).

Conflict Can Be a Motivator for Change Within Yourself

If you are willing to examine how you've handled conflict both today and in the past, you can identify certain behavioral characteristics in your communication skills that can lead to effective change.

Conflict Can Help Build Relationships

Sounds kind of contradictory, right? However, when you manage your differences in a positive way, it's possible to strengthen your relationship with your boss, peers, and others because of your willingness to work things out. Bad feelings may be interpreted differently after further discussion, often resulting in a change in your perception of others and their perception of you.

Conflict Will Not Go Away By Itself

That would be nice wouldn't it? But the truth is conflict rarely disappears on its own. It takes the effort of both sides to manage the situation into a working relationship.

Conflict Doesn't Have to Result in a Winner and a Loser

Although winning and losing is sometimes the case, through the effective use of interpersonal skill, conflict management can result in a win/win, compromise, or collaboration agreement with neither party losing.

Conflict Should Not Be Suppressed

You certainly don't want to continually raise conflict, but suppressing it doesn't make it go away. Usually it serves only to build additional barriers between people. It's much more effective to deal with it when it occurs.

Five Methods of Managing Conflict

Most people have a tendency to deal with conflict the same way each time it happens. In fact, you should vary your approach to managing conflict just as you vary your approach in dealing with different people.

There are two things for you to consider before determining which method to use:

- Who is the other person involved?
- What is the situation?

Following are five methods you can choose from after considering the individual and the situation. Each is appropriate in certain instances.

Competing (or, "I win, you lose")

Competing is an attempt to dominate; it is a winner-take-all position. It is also a power-based mode where you use whatever you can to win the situation, such as your ability to argue or perhaps your rank in the organization.

Usually when this approach is used, the focus is on winning at all costs rather than searching for the most appropriate solution for everyone involved. These characteristics may lead you to believe that competing would rarely be useful in the workplace. However, there are times when this win/lose approach is appropriate.

When to Use Competing

• **When quick, decisive action is necessary.** There will be times when you have to make decisions that will override another's point of view. As long as it doesn't become habitual, you're probably okay.

• **When unpopular changes need to be implemented.** Consider the latest policy to come down from on high. You may not like it and others may not either, but there's no choice in the matter. Like it or not, everyone has to live by it.

• **When other methods have been tried and failed.** This may involve working with others who are not being cooperative. Sometimes, despite your efforts to work things out in other ways, you may have to pull rank.

If you use competing as the method to manage your conflict, you must also determine to win at the expense of the other party losing. Making this choice shouldn't be easy because you run the risk of hurting the working relationship.

A word of caution: Be extremely careful about using this approach with your boss. It may not be too healthy for your future.

Accommodation (or, "I lose, you win")

Accommodation is the opposite of competing. Using this approach indicates you are willing to give in to another's wishes or position.

To be used properly, accommodation should come from an assertive decision rather than a nonassertive habit. This method can be very helpful at times, especially when you're attempting to build a good relationship. Of course to overuse it wouldn't be good because it would indicate weakness on your part. But when chosen appropriately, using accommodation teaches us that sometimes it's best to let others have their way.

When to Use Accommodation

• **When it's more important to preserve the relationship rather than argue the issue.** There will be times when you have to weigh the importance of the issue against the risk of hurting the relationship. Husbands and wives do it all the time. Sometimes the issue simply isn't worth the risk.

• **When the issue is more important to the other person than it is to you.** This is a perfect example of choosing accommodation. Another person may attach a certain importance to a particular issue that you could go either way on. Go ahead, give in.

• **When you want to encourage others to learn through self-discovery.** Even if you know there's a better way, sometimes it's best to let others learn certain things on their own. For example, you might ask someone to do something for you but allow him or her to choose the method rather than explaining everything step by step.

• **When you realize you're wrong.** Amazingly, people seldom admit they're wrong even when they know they are.

Avoidance (or, "I lose, you lose")

On the surface, avoidance appears to be inappropriate for resolving differences. It is referred to as the lose/lose outcome because neither party chooses to deal with the issue.

Sometimes, however, avoidance can help resolve differences between two people. For example, in the heat of an argument, temporary avoidance or diffusion can give both you and the other person time to calm down. Later the two of you can take up the issue again.

When this approach is used, it's important that the person who asks for the "time out" brings up the issue again within an appropriate amount of time. Failure to do so could be perceived as a manipulative ploy used to ignore or avoid the issue entirely. And that just makes the situation wore.

When to Use Avoidance

• **When the issue is trivial to both parties.** Some things just aren't worth arguing about. If an issue isn't important to you or the other person, simply let it go.

• **When others can resolve the conflict more effectively.** It's important to know when to stay out of things. Sometimes others may be just as adept as you in resolving certain issues. In fact, usually the fewer people involved in a disagreement, the greater the chances are for a solution.

• **When raising the issue may do more damage than leaving it alone.** Sometimes raising a previously unresolved or sensitive issue may do more harm than good. If you think this may be the case, it may be better to let it be.

Compromise (or, "I win and lose some; you win and lose some")

The compromise approach involves negotiation, trade-offs, swapping, and a high degree of flexibility. It is referred to as the win/lose–win/lose position because although you will get some of what you want, you also have to give up something in the process.

It's important to decide in advance how much you're willing to give away before you begin to negotiate. In other words, you need to set limits. This doesn't necessarily mean you'll have to give away everything up to that point; setting limits in advance simply gives you a range within which you can negotiate effectively.

When using compromise to manage differences, you indicate your concern not only for your own objectives but also for maintaining the relationship. Compromise is an attempt to find the common ground of agreement.

When to Use Compromise

• **When searching for a common ground to competing goals and equal power.** Competing goals indicate a win/lose outcome. If both of you have competing goals and equal power, neither of you can win. The best thing to do is to focus on the give-and-take approach.

• **When you need temporary settlement to complex matters.** Many issues are too difficult to settle all at once, especially when time is of the essence. Compromise attempts to reach agreement for the moment, until further negotiations can take place.

• **When maintaining the relationship and reaching an agreement are equally important.** Winning everything but hurting or even losing a relationship in the process is hardly worth the price, especially because you'll probably have to deal with that person again. With compromise, you at least get some of what you want while giving the other person part of what he or she needs.

Collaboration (or, "I win, you win")

Collaboration is usually considered the best (and the most difficult) approach to managing conflict because there is a maximum concern for both the issues and the relationship. Collaboration also attempts to establish a climate that enables you and the other person to examine and understand each other's point of view. It is referred to as win/win because it involves identifying those areas where agreements exist and where there are differences, evaluating alternatives, and selecting solutions that have full support and commitment.

This kind of problem solving requires trust, the surfacing of hidden agendas, and a willingness to be creative in order to reach resolution.

There are three critical conditions that must be satisfied in order to reach collaboration.

• *Willingness to resolve.* Both of you must be willing to resolve the issue; you can't do it alone. Any hidden agendas or failure to trust or to be honest will prevent the outcome you want.

• *Willingness to go to the root problem.* Often what appears to be the problem is only a symptom of the real issue. Both of you must be willing to explore the origins of the conflict in order to identify its true source and deal with it.

• *Willingness to empathize.* Feelings are always a part of conflict. Both of you must be willing to accept and understand each other's feelings and point of view, even though you may not agree with the other. Agreement isn't the issue. The point is to accept, understand, and validate each other's feelings.

When to Use Collaboration
• When both of you are willing to explore alternatives that neither of you had thought of individually. You've heard it before: Two heads are better than one. Perhaps you've both brought ideas to the table. Perhaps neither of you is able to convince the other. Perhaps you can't find a compromise. This may be the time

to go for the collaborative effort and together develop a totally new approach.

• **When you want to merge experiences and feelings from people who have different backgrounds and perspectives.** Sometimes when attempting to work out differences, it's helpful to gather others' opinions to help sort things out and perhaps discover a different point of view.

• **When you want to get at unresolved root problems that may have hindered the working relationship over a long period of time.** Is there someone in your organization with whom you've had an ongoing conflict? If so, you may want to try collaboration to see if the two of you can resolve the issue. Of course, someone has to go first . . . and you're the one who's reading this book.

Summary

We know that conflict will occur in the workplace because it is a natural human dynamic. But that isn't the point. The real issue is how you manage it when it happens.

Remember these characteristics of conflict:

- It is inevitable.
- It can be productive or destructive, depending on how you handle it.
- Not all conflicts will be resolved, but most can be managed.
- Conflict can be a motivator for change.
- It can help build relationships.
- Conflict will not go away by itself.
- It doesn't have to result in a winner and a loser.
- It should be dealt with rather than suppressed.

To deal with conflict, you have at least five possible alternatives to choose from.

Competing (win/lose)

- When quick, decisive action is necessary
- When unpopular changes need to be implemented
- When other methods have been tried and failed

Accommodation (lose/win)

- When it's more important to preserve the relationship rather than argue the issue
- When the issue is more important to the other person than to yourself
- When you want to encourage others to learn through self-discovery
- When you realize you're wrong

Avoidance (lose/lose)

- When the issue is trivial to both parties
- When others can resolve the conflict more effectively
- When raising the issue may do more harm than good

Compromise (win/lose–win/lose)

- When searching for a common ground to competing goals and equal power
- When you need temporary settlement to complex issues
- When maintaining relationship and reaching an agreement are equally important

Collaboration (win/win)

- When both of you are willing to explore alternatives that neither of you had thought of individually
- When you want to merge experiences and feelings from people who have different backgrounds and perspectives
- When you want to get at unresolved root problems, that may have hindered the working relationship over a long period of time

Index

About the Author

Jerry Wisinski is a management and communications consultant living in San Antonio, Texas. He was an adjunct professor at Trinity University and was formerly the executive director of International Trainers, Educators, and Consultants. He is also a course developer and seminar leader for the American Management Association International. He is the author of *Resolving Conflicts on the Job* (AMACOM, 1993).